CALDICOT
AND THE VILLAGES OF THE MOOR
in Old Photographs
including PORTSKEWETT, SUDBROOK,
ROGGIETT, LLANVIHANGEL, MAGOR,
UNDY, ON THE LEVELS &
AROUND AND ABOUT NETHERWENT

by
Richard D. Jones

Volume 2

This book is dedicated to the memory of my father,
Malcolm D. Jones

Foreword by
David Davies
M.P. for Monmouth

Old Bakehouse Publications

Abertillery

First published in November 2007

ISBN 978-1-905967-08-7

Published in the U.K. by
Old Bakehouse Publications
Church Street,
Abertillery, Gwent NP13 1EA
Telephone: 01495 212600 Fax: 01495 216222
Email: theoldbakeprint@btconnect.com
Website: www.oldbakehouseprint.co.uk

Made and printed in the UK
by J.R. Davies (Printers) Ltd.

British Library Cataloguing in Publication Data: a catalogue
record for this book is available from the British Library.

Foreword

by

David Davies, M.P.

When Richard Jones asked me to write an introduction to the second volume of Caldicot and the Villages of the Moor I was delighted to oblige.

We live in a fast moving world in which people move about the country (and often away from it) in pursuit of their careers. When living life at this pace it is easy to lose the sense of historical contact with the areas we live in; a sense that came automatically to those who could trace back generations of ancestors living in the same place.

Richard has a gift for using photographs and stories to enable us to see the area of southern Monmouthshire through the eyes of those who went before us. In doing so the reader becomes aware that local history is not the study of some far off land which is irrelevant to the present. Rather, it is a look at the lives of the people who helped to make this area what it is today.

Whether the reader has lived in Monmouthshire all their life, or is just visiting, each page will be a joy to turn. But this book should not simply be a pleasant reminiscence about the past, but a warning for the future. The pages about the 'Great Flood' are as relevant to those living on the levels today as they have been for the generations who continued to live and farm here after the waters of 1607 had receded.

The rise in sea levels predicted to take place over the next century has not yet been matched by a rise in funds for sea defences. This book offers a warning of what could happen and what we stand to lose if we are not prepared to take action to protect this beautiful corner of Monmouthshire.

But I am an optimist. Generations have toiled away to make southern Monmouthshire one of the most pleasant corners of our land and it is a heritage we will not throw away. The following pages will introduce us to a few of those characters and their stories. I am sure that others will enjoy reading it as much as I did.

David T C Davies

HOUSE OF COMMONS

Contents

FOREWORD

INTRODUCTION

Introduction

It seems like only yesterday that Caldicot & the Villages of the Moor - Volume One, was published. Yet incredibly thirteen years have passed and much has changed.

Only a few years following the publication of Volume One in 1995, my father, Malcolm Jones died suddenly, aged just 49 years. This new book - Volume Two - is dedicated to his memory. Volume Two was always an unspoken intention of his.

The huge sales success of Volume One (having now been re-printed on several occasions) bears witness to the high degree of interest and enthusiasm for all matters of local history. Postcards and photographs convey in a unique way the social history and changing landscapes of the late nineteenth and twentieth centuries. Such changes are perhaps more pronounced and more frequent in an area such as south Monmouthshire, where sustained periods of economic prosperity have led to new development and re-development throughout history. Such pressures for change continue today.

Volume Two contains over two hundred images, many of them private photographs which have never been published before. Additionally, in a change from Volume One, I have taken the decision to include two further chapters. Chapter Five includes images of the villages on the western part of the Caldicot Levels, such as Nash, Goldcliff, Whitson & Llanwern, whilst Chapter Six includes a journey through some of the other villages of Netherwent from Langstone in the west, to Mathern in the east.

I hope that readers of this latest volume will find enjoyment in rekindling memories of years past, or for those who have more recently made this area their home, that they might find pleasure in discovering something of the rich and fascinating history that surrounds them.

My heartfelt thanks to all the staff at Old Bakehouse Publications for their professional expertise involved in bringing this project to fruition and to my partner Joanne for her support and patience during long hours of research and collation.

Richard D Jones
Caerwent, Monmouthshire
October 2007

CHAPTER 1
Caldicot

1. A high old time at Caldicot c.1910.
This is a card typical of the Edwardian period. This example illustrates a gentleman evidently dressed for a holiday, who is looking forward to leaving behind him his work in the factories, to enjoy a high old time in Caldicot. Card designs like this one were sold to a local retailer (often a local Post Office) and a quantity overprinted with a local message and place name.

2. The Cross, Caldicot c.1960.

A meeting of the hunt pictured here at The Cross. It was obviously still safe to meet at what is now a busy road junction! The newer police station can be seen in the background, having replaced the former one located directly opposite on Chepstow Road. The roundabout seen here was constructed in 1938, presumably to cope with the increasing popularity of the motor car. The roundabout arrangement continued until c.1990 when the road junction was re-modelled as part of the town centre pedestrian scheme.

3. The Cross, Caldicot 1957.

Another view of the much photographed Caldicot Cross. On the immediate left can be seen the stables of 'The White Hart' Inn, here advertising 'Lloyds Ales & Stout'. In the centre of the scene is Beaufort House, formerly 'The Beaufort' Inn, which along with its neighbours 'The Cross' and 'The White Hart' made for a good selection of public houses all gathered around The Cross! Several generations of the Squibbs family occupied Beaufort House from the late 1800s and for the first half of the 20th century. The Post Office/telephone exchange attached to the right of the main property and Beaufort House itself, were a hub of activity for parish life - not least because several generations of the Squibbs family were postmasters, local undertakers and builders and also clerks to the parish council. Villagers could call in to send a telegram. The exchange opened in 1923 and had a battery operated switchboard! There was a total of eight private telephones in the village at the time! Beyond the Post Office was located for sometime the Chalet Café operated by Roly Williams (also newsagents at separate premises).

4. Messrs Squibbs 1906 invoice.

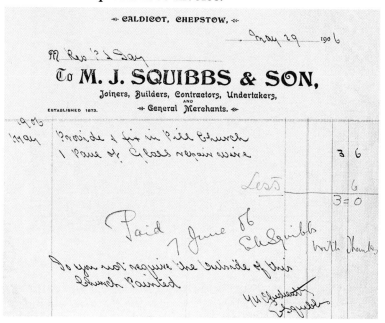

An invoice from Messrs Squibbs to Revd P. Day for St Michael's church, The Pill, Caldicot, for the repair of a broken pane of glass and for fixing wire - and we think vandalism is a trait of today! Complaints about the behaviour of the boys from The Pill had already been made. Indeed bad behaviour from Caldicot boys was reported to the parish council in 1895 and they considered what steps should be taken in connection with recent bad behaviour in St Mary's churchyard. Note the letterhead - as was often the case builders and joiners were also local undertakers - as were the Squibbs family. Also note the interesting footnote from Mr Squibbs - *'Do you not require the outside of this church painted?'* A less than subtle attempt by Mr Squibbs to obtain further work for himself?

5. Messrs Squibbs invoice 1906.

And here's another invoice that gives us an insight into the work of Messrs Squibbs and which perhaps says something about village life in the early 1900s. This invoice is to Caldicot parish church c/o Revd F. Clarke. More vandalism deterrents were obviously required! This invoice for repairing the churchyard wall, cementing top copings and fixing glass on same. Squibbs also repaired the lychgate and fitted a padlock and provided two keys for the same. Presumably these were to lock the churchyard each night to try and deter the troublemakers! Note the date on the top of the invoice - *'established 1873'*. The Squibbs family were prominent in Caldicot village life for over a hundred years.

6. The Cross, Caldicot c.1900.
Another photograph of The Cross showing both the White Hart and The Cross public houses together. The picture has a rural feel - although notice the policeman is on duty outside the pubs in case of trouble! A medieval preaching cross remained here until the mid 1800s - Wesley is said to have preached at it. This is quite an early picture - certainly before 1906 because in that year a large gas lamp was erected by the parish council in the street in front of The White Hart. This photograph shows just how narrow Sandy Lane was, a tight squeeze between the two pubs!

7. The White Hart.
Pictured in the winter snow of 1968, shortly before its demolition and replacement a year later. Despite all the town centre redevelopment the telephone box remains largely in the same position even today! Attached to the side of The White Hart was a function or committee room requisitioned in WWII as a depot for the local civil defence force. A 1901 advertisement describes the White Hart as *'restored and replete with every comfort'* (Kelly's directory 1901). In the early 1900s the landlord was recorded as one *'W Jenkins'*.

MONMOUTHSHIRE.

CALDICOT and ROGGIETT.

Particulars, with Plan, of Important Sale of

105 ACRES

OF

FREEHOLD AND COPYHOLD

LANDS & PREMISES

COMPRISING—

Farm Residence & Outbuildings, Cottages & Gardens,

and Pasture, Arable, & Building Lands,

WHICH

MESSRS. DAVIS, NEWLAND & HUNT

have received instructions from the Representatives of the late Mr. WM. BENNETT, to

SELL BY AUCTION,

AT THE

WHITE HART HOTEL, CALDICOT,

On THURSDAY, JUNE 13th, 1895,

at THREE o'clock in the afternoon, subject to the Conditions of Sale of the Monmouthshire Incorporated Law Society, and such Special Conditions as shall be then read.

For further particulars apply to the Auctioneers, WELSH STREET, CHEPSTOW, & HIGHBURY, MBERS, NEWPORT, or to

Messrs. FRANCIS, STANTON, & PARNALL, Solicitors, Newport.
Messrs. MORGAN, FRANCIS, & STANTON, Solicitors, Chepstow.

MULLOCK AND SONS PRINTERS, NEWPORT

8. Property Auction poster 1895. Villagers in Caldicot on June 13th 1895 might have gone to the function room of The White Hart and would have witnessed the auction of a farmhouse, outbuildings and 105 acres of agricultural land at Caldicot and Roggiett, by auctioneers Davies, Newland & Hunt. After various mergers the auctioneers are still in existence today.

9. The Cross, Caldicot 1957.
Pictured here is W.J. Evans chemist - now the New Garden Chinese take-away. The former public toilets can also be seen. Evans the family chemist opened 1934 and offered a van delivery service for urgent orders. As well as selling the usual range of chemist's goods, they sold a full range of spirits - presumably for medicinal purposes!

10. Caldicot village c.1880.

This is one of the earliest photographs included in this volume, perhaps from as early as 1880. Home-made cheese or butter are being sold from the table in front of the cottages here. This scene looks towards The Cross, the building now occupied by Wye Valley Studios being on the centre left of the photograph. The small cottages on the immediate left of the photograph were of great age and Thomas Birbeck (in his book *'From village to town'*) described them as *'small and whitewashed, where you stepped down from the road straight into the front room'*. A later picture shows one of the other cottages was also a shop of sorts displaying the sign *'Pride Confectioners'*. If you look at the side of the Wye Valley Studio's buildings today, you can still see the outline of the roof of the former cottages. They were demolished in 1969 for the redevelopment of the town centre, to be replaced by Liptons supermarket, also now just a memory.

11. Caldicot village centre c.1955.

This picture shows that Caldicot was a small, but busy retail centre for the village population and for the other villages of the area. On the right of the picture were located the gas showrooms, whilst above was Francis' furniture shop. Further along on the right were the labour exchange and The Strand, whilst located on the left, readers may remember R.J.C. Francis & Co. (Grocers) whose 1963 advert included the strange combination of *'Bird's Eye frozen food & home furnishings for dining, lounge and bedroom suites!'* On the immediate left of the scene is Washbourne's Ironmongers located in the original Wesleyan Chapel. Cyril Washbourne began by selling bicycles and later added a shop and garage. This original chapel was built as early as 1810 and continued in use until the current Methodist Chapel was built in 1895. The original chapel retained its balcony and pulpit for many years. Following the relocation of the chapel the original premises became a reading room for the young men of the village, owned by Mrs Holmes. Her intention was that this facility would provide activity for the young men of the village many of whom were unemployed during the depression years of the 1920s and 1930s. Beyond here was a tin hut, where at one time there was a hairdressers and beyond this stables used by *'Fishy Davies'*. Many of the buildings shown here were demolished a decade or so later when the shopping centre was redeveloped and expanded. The Edwardian terrace of houses (far right of photograph) and Beaufort House (distant centre of photograph) were the only buildings fortunate to survive this fate.

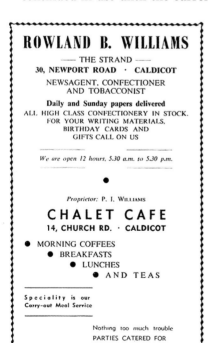
12. Rowland B Williams - 1963 advertisement.

Like numerous other local traders, Rowland Williams had interests in several concerns and here he advertises them in a 1963 local directory. The speciality of the Chalet Café is advertised as a *'carry-out meal service'*. Was this Caldicot's first take-away?

13. F.H. Cole - Ironmongers c.1920.
An evocative period photograph of the Caldicot Plumbing & Ironmongery Company. Located on the site where Mills newsagents is today, a first floor was later added to the back part of the newsagents and now appears to form part of the row of rather imposing houses, but is in fact a later addition to the row. Is this Mr Francis Cole (Proprietor) and his children in this photograph? Look at the huge quantity and variety of hardware on display in the shop windows! Francis Cole was leader of the Caldicot civil defence rescue party during WWII. He was also president of George V Silver Jubilee Committee charged with arranging the parish jubilee celebrations in 1935.

14./15. F.H. Cole (Ironmongers) invoices.
Here are two of F.H. Cole's letterheads - quite elaborate, as was the style of business stationery at the time. The first invoice on the left is one from F.H. Cole to Caldicot Parish Church - church yard account, dated 1911 and is for supplying a grass shears and scythe. Cutting the churchyard is a large enough task today even with powered machinery, but just imagine cutting it with a shears and scythe! The second invoice

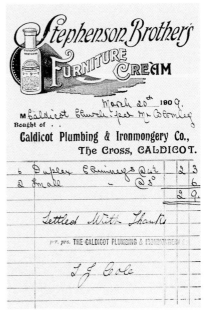

(on the right) is one for 6 duplex chimneys and 2 smaller chimneys (for oil lamps), to Caldicot church c/o Mr Blomley, who was churchwarden and also headmaster of the village church school.

16. Chepstow Road, Caldicot 1957.
Many readers will remember George Lewis, butcher at 19 Chepstow Road, here on the left of the picture. Even in the late 1950s Caldicot is largely unaltered - a quiet rural village where it was safe to play on the roads and cycle without danger. Although the road has been slightly re-aligned and straightened, this scene is otherwise largely unchanged today.

17. S H Adams & Sons advertisement 1963.

Adams' shop - more correctly S.H. Adams & Son, was founded by Samuel Hill Adams who was born in 1833, son of William Adams of West End, Caldicot. Originally a butcher and greengrocer and later a fishmonger too, the business was located at London House, Chepstow Road, Caldicot. In the 1901 Kelly's directory S.H. Adams are also listed as Milliner's. *'Best terms for cash'* said the company advert. Adams' shop front was said to be the finest in Caldicot. An E.R. Adams of Caldicot is listed as a market gardener and he was elected to the first Caldicot Parish Council in 1894 and also to the rural district council. In 1963 the shop was also a drapers and sold schoolwear for Caldicot Village College. The business served Caldicot for many years, including delivery to your door by means of the shop bicycle! Adams ceased trading on June 30th 1982 and is now partly occupied by Blatchley's funeral directors and partly by a baguette shop.

18. An early advertisement of Henry Jones for self raising flour.

Court House Farm is one of Caldicot's oldest private dwellings and although now surrounded by the Castle Lea housing estate, the property has great significance in the history of Caldicot. It has a particular retail importance, but it is of much greater age, originally being a farm to the castle during the middle ages. Henry Jones was a young farmer from Undy and the son of a corn dealer. He married Ann Pride at Llanvihangel Roggiett church in November 1838 and they came to live at Court House which they inherited from Ann's aunt. Shortly after marriage Henry started in business as a purveyor of flour and maker of biscuits at Bristol. He had perfected and patented a method of making self raising flour and as such, being the first in this field, he achieved world wide success. By 1852 he had licensees in Australia, the United States and New Zealand. Queen Victoria was an early user and he was

appointed royal purveyor of flour and biscuits to Her Majesty. So Caldicot can justly claim to be the home of self raising flour!

19. A selection of local advertisements from 1963.

By 1963 the development of Caldicot as a *'new town'* was well underway. Consequently the number of new retailers and small businesses was burgeoning. Numerous have long since closed, but many readers will have fond memories of shopping in Caldicot in these *'pioneering'* times. The rather imaginative connection within the advertisement for *'The Castle Inn'* of Caldicot Castle with a quote from Shakespeare's *'Macbeth'* is historically without foundation, but nevertheless is perhaps a slick marketing idea!

20. The Triangle, Sandy Lane, Caldicot - advertisement.

At *'The Haywain'* public house during the 1970s, would have been found *'The Triangle Cinema'*. Here's an advert from the 1973 showing of *'Gold'* with Roger Moore and Susannah York. This was not the first cinema in Caldicot - others were at Church Road and also Chepstow Road, the latter showing silent films during the 1920s, when accompaniment was provided by Mr Harris' harmonium, brought up from The Pill, for the occasion.

21. Fieldgate Cottage, Sandy Lane c.1950.
Thomas Birbeck (*'From village to town'*) says that the public highway went as far as Fieldgate Cottage, where at one time there was a gate providing access to Great Field or Common Field (Cae Mawr in Welsh). When the fields were enclosed in 1859 Sandy Lane became the only access to the fields, but the road was not taken over and maintained by any authority. Its condition and the state of the hedgerows were troublesome for many years as recorded in minutes of the parish council meetings.

22. From the garden of Fieldgate Cottage, Sandy Lane c.1950.
This picture looks down Sandy Lane towards The Cross. Here can be seen the back elevation of the then White Hart Inn. On the right of this scene - in the early 1900s - were allotments which formed part of the Herbert Charity land, detailed on a large painted bequest board in Caldicot parish church.

23. Joseph Stell Esq.

John Stell (who was born in 1792) was the manager of a cotton mill at Sedbergh, Yorkshire and when he retired he accompanied his married son Joseph to Caldicot. Joseph was very versatile and proficient in a number of trades. He was engaged by Henry Hughes in 1862 to lay down the plant for the new wire works being installed at The Pill, Caldicot. He also carried out work for the wire works at Tintern. As soon as he arrived in Caldicot he purchased a plot of land in Sandy Lane upon which he erected his house. He also constructed a row of dwellings in Sandy Lane and more at Highmoor Hill and Tintern. When work was about to start on the Severn Tunnel, Joseph Stell anticipated that there would be a great demand for bread and so, in 1875, he built on his site in Sandy Lane, the most modern bakery in the county. Stells were then in a position to cater adequately for the increasing population. Joseph was a popular person in the village. He was well known as a keeper of bees and he was a pillar of the Wesleyan community. He was an outstanding figure in his long frock-tailed coat, white waistcoat, spats and tall top hat. Every Friday it was his custom to go to Newport and return with a large quantity of sweets which he parcelled up in bags and gave to the children. Several more successive generations carried on the business until its demise just a few years ago.

24. Church Road, Caldicot c.1948.

Porretta's van will serve you an ice cream! Here pictured on Church Road possibly in the late 1940s.

25. Newport Road, Caldicot c.1910.
An unusual street scene looking along Newport Road towards Pantile Row and Yew Tree Terrace. The row of cottages on the left side, in the distance, were called Woodbine Cottages. Pantile Row (first row of houses on right side) was built first and is featured on a 1902 map - the name reflecting the original style of roof tile fitted to the cottages. Yew Tree Terrace (beyond) was built some time shortly after 1902. It is strange to think of these houses pictured here as being just a few years old! On the right of the picture there is a small shop located on the very end of the terrace - now the location of a veterinary surgery. The premises were owned by one C. Watkins and dealt in bicycle sales and repairs.

26. Newport Road, Caldicot 1957.
The frontage of Longcroft Farm is seen here on the left of the picture. It was more commonly known as *'Gwillims Farm'* after its farmer occupants - The Gwillim family. On the immediate left, is now located The Good Measure public house. The row of three cottages in the distant left have also been demolished where now stands Waghausel Close. Note the three shops on the right largely unaltered today. In 1963 here you would have found W.L. Ford greengrocers, (general supplies and frozen foods) and a little beyond Mesdames Gleed & Coggins in B & J Fashions. Perhaps these names bring back memories for some readers?

27. Caldicot Sewerage Treatment Works c.1965.
Drainage issues occupied a great deal of Caldicot Parish Council's time during the first half of the twentieth century. In 1908 the Parish Council suggested to the local authority that the primitive drainage systems should be connected to Dowles drain. This was a wide culvert below Ifton Manor Farm, which then passed directly and untreated into the river Severn. The work was eventually completed in 1920s. The works you see here were opened in 1965 (this photograph probably dates from the opening) by the Rural District Council. This coincided with the expansion of Caldicot and the new plant was designed for an eventual population of 17,000 people.

28. Church Road, Caldicot c.1951.
Watch out for the cyclists! On the right of this scene there were previously located two wooden huts. One was the YMCA building, but another was bought from the Beachley Army camp by Colonel Cummins of Caldicot Hall, for use by the unemployed men of the village during the Depression. It proved a successful venture, but by 1938 was no longer needed, so was handed over to the village as a parish hall. During the period 1941-1958, during war time and rationing afterwards, it was converted into a *'British Restaurant'*. The District Council had the idea of offering wholesome meals, to nourish the local population from the meagre rations available. Adaptions were made to the hall and the charge was 1/6d (7½p)for a meal.

29. Caldicot Halt c.1935.

Not a very impressive sight to welcome the traveller! The first Caldicot Halt was constructed of re-used railway sleepers, but nonetheless was a great boon for the local population. Thomas Birbeck in his book *'Caldicot from village to town'* wrote: *'In May 1932 the GWR informed the parish council saying they were going to place a halt at Benacre and it opened in September of that year'*. For locals this avoided the lengthy walk to Severn Tunnel Junction or Portskewett. British Rail made several attempts to close the halt during various rationalization programmes, but it survives to this day.

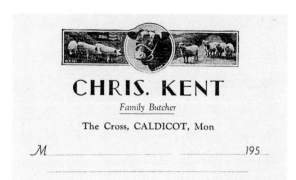

CHRIS. KENT

Family Butcher

The Cross, CALDICOT, Mon

M..195....

....

30. C. Kent (Butcher) Church Road, Caldicot.
Another popular independent Caldicot butcher was Chris Kent - here's one of his original letterheads. His premises were located at Church Road and are now occupied by '*A Touch of Class*'.

31. Church Road, Caldicot 1963.
Struggling through the snow in the winter of 1963 in Church Road. Is that someone cycling through the snow?

32. Off Church Road, Caldicot c.1933.
Pictured here Miss Grace Shepherd (later Williams) parked up behind what later became known as The Coach House of Dr. Walford Davies. You can see St Mary's church clearly in the background. The author isn't aware that Miss Shepherd ever took a driving test!

33. The Castle Inn c.1950.

The Castle Inn - almost certainly Caldicot's oldest public house. Today it's a *'free house'* although for a considerable time it was a *'Hancock's'* pub. Although extended to the back, the frontage has changed little and it is a pleasant reminder of *'old Caldicot'* forming part of an attractive group of properties gathered around the ancient church and castle.

34. The Castle Inn - Landlady c.1958.

For many years if you had walked into The Castle Inn at Caldicot, standing behind the bar would almost certainly have been this lady. Mrs. Dodd was landlady of The Castle Inn for over 60 years and died only a short time after retiring at the great age of 88 in the 1960s.

35. Caldicot Castle driveway c.1930.
A walk along the driveway of Caldicot Castle between the two world wars would have offered you a view rather like this one. Here you can see a World War One German gun, presented to Caldicot parish, but which caused much embarrassment as a home could not be found for it and it ended up languishing in a ditch near the Tippling Philosopher Inn. Eventually Mrs Cobb of Caldicot Castle had it rescued and erected on a plinth on the castle drive. It remained here until it was melted down for scrap towards the war effort in World War Two.

36. Caldicot Castle 1910.
In this scene large areas of fields surrounding the castle are flooded - quite a common occurrence in former years. This photograph is dated February 1910. Readers should note that it is evident that large sections of the castle walls have yet to be restored by the owner Mr. Cobb. No doubt the original, natural floodplains of the Neddern Brook were welcome additions to the already impressive man-made defences of this ancient stronghold.

37. Caldicot Castle 1913.
This picture is one of a series that illustrate the work of excavating the original moat around the castle which over many centuries had become filled with rubble, earth and undergrowth. This photograph shows a scene outside the Woodstock tower. Notice the small tramway which was laid around large sections of the moat to facilitate removal of the waste spoil.

38. Caldicot Castle Gardens c.1908.
It was a rare treat for villagers to have been allowed a peek inside the castle when it was a home to the Cobb family. Pictured here are the gardens and borders presented in pristine order, along with productive vegetable patches, all maintained by Mr. John Dickinson, who was sometime gardener to the Cobbs and later to the Rural District Council after they bought the castle in 1963.

39. Caldicot Castle auction advertisement 1963.

On Friday 11th October 1963 an auction sale was happening at Caldicot Castle. It comprised the contents of the castle belonging to the Cobb family, on their sale of the property to the Rural District Council. The description of some of the items allows them to be recognised as being those which remain in the few furnished rooms of the castle to this day. The council was successful in buying back some of the furniture allowing it to be retained within the castle.

40. Pill Row, Caldicot c.1900.

A scene that has changed beyond all recognition. Here Pill Row looks to be a leafy rural location - indeed the location for a leisurely afternoon walk. Pill Row led to an area known either as Beesditch or Carterstown, the latter after Mr. Timothy Carter who owned the land on the other side of the railway line.

41. Caldicot Crossing signal box c.1900.
The works in the background of the picture look derelict at this point. The fortunes of the business frequently ebbed and flowed and there were several prolonged periods of closure. It was first founded as a wire works by Henry Hughes in 1862. By 1898 business was obviously poor and the receivers were appointed and all work stopped. In 1909 William Thomas bought the works and restarted it as the Caldicot Tin Stamping Works. This picture almost certainly pre-dates his acquisition at a time when the factory was idle. Mr. Baggaley was the works manager in the 1930s and took a leading part in Caldicot village life. He was treasurer to the Jubilee Committee in 1935, but later left the district. Mr. Luff was also at sometime manager and he too played a significant role in local affairs. Parts of the works were sold in 1945 to the Avon Aluminium Company. The cottages behind were originally built for workers constructing the Severn tunnel in the 1870s. Formerly there was a much greater population at Beesditch, but many of the properties have since been demolished.

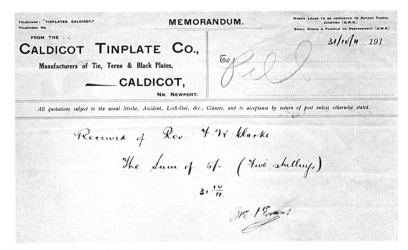

42. Caldicot Tin Plate Works - Receipt 1911.
A receipt to Rev. F.W. Clarke, vicar of Caldicot, for payment to the works of five shillings, dated 31st October 1911. Might have this been in connection with supplying material for repairs to the nearby iron church of St Michael and All Angels?

43. Tin Plate works group September 1935.

This photograph was taken on the occasion of Mr. Baggaley's retirement as manager of the Caldicot Tin Plate Works in September 1935. Here pictured are (seated) Mr and Mrs Baggaley and (standing) Kathleen and Dorothy whose surnames are unknown to the author.

44. Britton's shop, Beesditch, Caldicot. c.1900.

Here at Beesditch, Britton's shop was located right alongside the railway. Beesditch was quite a community of its own and its people were fiercely independent and proud. St Michaels and All Angels church was erected in 1894 (of corrugated iron construction). This wasn't evidently a huge success for in 1923 the decision was made to re-locate the entire church building to Church Road, Caldicot, where it served as the church hall until as recently as 1980 - where many of us received our Sunday school lessons! There were two more buildings of corrugated iron construction. One a Sunday school (operated by Mrs. Dally the owner of a well known Caldicot sweet shop), but also used for mothers' meetings every Tuesday, these organised by Mrs. Cropper of nearby Mount Ballan. It was later converted into a bungalow. The third building was partly a dwelling, with a large room attached, for a time used for non-conformist worship.

45. Caldicot Castle no. 4074 c.1955.
The steam locomotive *'Caldicot Castle'* no. 4074 was built in December 1923 and was first based at the Old Oak Common engine sheds. It took part in speed trials in 1925. Between August 1950 and March 1959 it was based at Landore, Swansea and regularly passed through Caldicot during that time and it is likely that this is when this photograph was taken. The locomotive was modified in 1959 and moved back to Old Oak Common. It was withdrawn from service in 1963 at the end of the steam era and later scrapped - a sad end for a magnificent engine. Ironically this was the same year that the Cobb family sold the actual castle - the end of an era for this community.

46. Caldicot Foreshore 1907.
At the beginning of the twentieth century the Severn Estuary was still a busy shipping channel. Incredibly strong tides and complex geography also made it one of the most treacherous - indeed it remains so. Here is a photograph of the ship *'Princess Waldermar'*, wrecked on Caldicot foreshore on 14th January 1907. Caldicot has a largely forgotten maritime history predominantly centred on Henry Wise of Caldicot Hall who built a series of ships at Caldicot in the 1700s. The former shipyard at Sudbrook also built several larger vessels. It was started by Thomas Walker to utilise some former workshops which had previously been used in the construction of the Severn Tunnel in the 1880s.

47. Caldicot AFC c.1902.
Little is known about this photograph other than the fact that pictured outside the former White Hart are the members of the Caldicot AFC team. Caldicot was home to numerous small football clubs, which along with the teams of other local villages competed in local leagues. Amongst others there were Caldicot Castle AFC (A and B teams), Tippling Philosopher AFC and Pill AFC.

48. St Mary's Parish Church group.
The Kings Messengers c.1912. Here pictured outside the former vicarage are: (Left to right) Back row: Doris Blomley, Dorothy Robbins, Unknown, Nellie Rymer, Unknown, Unknown, Unknown, Unknown, Unknown, Marjorie Evans, Unknown, Beatie James. Front row: ? Bolton, ? Lewis, Albert Evans, Unknown.

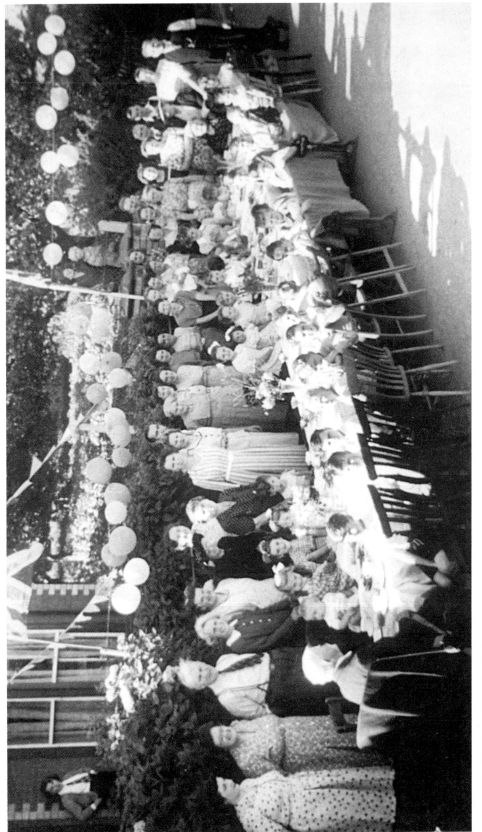

49. Station Road 1953.
This photograph was taken on the occasion of the 1953 coronation and shows a street party in Station Road. Amongst the many gathered for this jolly occasion are David Michael, Raymond Williams and Amy Margarets.

50./51. The Manchester Odd Fellows.

The Odd Fellows were very strong in Caldicot and their annual fête was held every August bank holiday from 1865 until the time of the First World War. They would typically commence the day with a church service and then proceed to the Tippling Philosopher (which was their headquarters) and after a dinner, they crossed the road to the Tippling field for sports and pony races. The whole village joined in proceedings which concluded with a dance in the Tippling hall.

The picture above is dated c.1905 and shows the Odd Fellows proceeding along Church Road to St Mary's Church for their annual service. The former St Mary's School is to be seen in the background.

The picture below shows the Odd Fellows gathered at Caldicot Cross in front of The White Hart in 1912.

52. The former Wesleyan Chapel.
The original Wesleyan Chapel was located a little further along Newport Road towards
The Cross, when compared to the site of the current chapel. It had been constructed
as early as 1810 and contained a gallery, pulpit and preaching desk which remained
features of the building long after its use as a chapel ceased. The building was
rendered redundant by the construction of the present chapel in 1895. This building
later became a village reading room, and later the home of Washbourne's
ironmongery store. The identities of the man and boy in the photograph are unknown.

53. The elders of the Wesleyan Chapel.
Sadly the author has been unable to identify individuals in this scene, but pictured are
the elders of The Wesleyan Methodist Chapel c.1930.

54. The Methodist Chapel Sisterhood.
The 'Sisterhood' has long been a feature of chapel life in Caldicot. Here pictured inside the chapel with their minister is a 'Sisterhood' group c.1950.

55. Church and School, Caldicot c.1900.
A truly rural scene looking across to the village school and parish church from the south, where today stands Castle Lea housing estate. Successive clergy paid for extensions to the school as the village grew and the population expanded. By the time this picture was taken the final extension to the building had been completed, this having been funded by Rev. F.W. Clarke (vicar) in the 1890s.

56. Parish Priest, Headmaster and teachers, St Mary's School, Caldicot. March 6th 1907. Pictured left to right: (Back row) Mrs. Prior, Hilda Jones, unknown, unknown, unknown, unknown (Front row) unknown, Rev F W Clarke, Rev Mathias (curate), Mr H Blomley (Headmaster).

57. Past Headmasters of St Mary's School c.1953.
Pictured are Mr Ellis Evans (left), Mr David Parry (right) and seated Mr Herbert Blomley. (Pictured outside the former school). In 1955 the senior pupils moved to the newly built Green Lane School and headmaster Mr. Ellis Evans transferred with them. However the infant pupils continued to be taught at St Mary's old school until 1968, when the current-day replacement St Mary's School was built and opened. The old school buildings were later demolished and housing built on the site.

58. St Mary's Parish Church c.1905.

A familiar view of St Mary's church, although a close look will show that subsequent to this photograph being taken the vestries to the north of the chancel were added (1911) - on this photograph they are absent. St Mary's has a small amount of Norman work, but dates chiefly from the 14th century. It is a large and elaborate church for what was once a small village. The tenor bell of the ring of eight bells within the church tower dates from 1450 having been originally cast by a Bristol bell-founder. It is in its original condition, having never been recast and sounds out Caldicot even today!

59. St Mary's Parish Church c.1910.

Here the inside of St Mary's church appears to have been decorated for Christmas - notice the holly around the capitals of the arches and on the window ledges. Oil lamps adorn the nave, but of course were for entirely practical purposes. The church walls were formerly plastered throughout and were painted with patterns and biblical texts. The plasterwork was removed c.1920 and the stonework of the walls exposed and pointed. Opinion is divided about which is the better look! The rood screen pictured here still exists, but was relocated to the rear (east) tower arch when the church was re-ordered in 1991. The church pews seen in this photograph were replaced by the current ones in the 1980s, the replacements having come from the closed church of St Luke, Bridge Street, Newport.

60. Dewstow House and Gardens, near Caldicot. c.1910.

In 1893, Mr. Henry Roger Keane Oakley became the owner of the Dewstow Estate, near Caldicot. Henry Oakley, or Squire Oakley as he was known locally, was a director of the Great Western Railway, but at home, he had two main interests. The first was the breeding of shire horses for which he established a reputation. All had names with the prefix of 'Dewstow'. His other main interest was the growing and cultivation of ferns, tropical flowers and plants.

Shortly after his arrival at Dewstow, he embarked on the creation of a garden which is remembered by some of the older generation in the area as a wondrous and magical place. Many of these folk remember an annual Sunday school outing to Dewstow, where they picnicked in the gardens at the invitation of Mr. Oakley. This was a garden, the like of which is not known to exist anywhere else. On the ground level, there were many rock gardens, ponds, water features, ornamental areas, tropical glass houses and a vast variety of plants, shrubs and trees from around the world.

It is only when you go below these gardens and you enter the subterranean world underneath, that you begin to understand the extent of the vision and enormous amount of work and skills involved in creating gardens that were unique at the turn of the 20th Century and may still be unique at the start of the 21st Century. Most of the surface gardens were filled in at various points over the years, but recent excavation has shown that what has been uncovered so far is in excellent condition and the gardens are now proving to be a highly popular visitor attraction.

CHAPTER 2

Portskewett & Sudbrook

61. Portskewett c.1902.

An early view of Portskewett village published by W A Call, The Wye Valley Studios, Chepstow. The former village stocks offer a convenient posing place for two local children. The stocks were formerly located on the roadside verge adjacent to the churchyard (as seen here), but were later removed to Chepstow Museum to protect them from the on-going enemies of age and weather.

62. Portskewett c.1950.

An original postcard published by the owner of Portskewett Post Office Z.I. Lewis. Kelly's trade directory of Monmouthshire 1901 includes the following in its entry for Portskewett - 'Post Office, MO & TO, TM O. Express Delivery, Parcel Post, S B & Annuity & Insurance Office, Portskewett - Miss Mary Kyte, sub-postmistress. Letters through Chepstow arrive at 7:45am, dispatched at 5:00pm & 6:35pm, Sundays 10:25am. Wall Letter Box at the Church, cleared at 4:25pm and 6:35 pm, Sundays, 10:20am.' Like many other small villages Portskewett has recently lost its village Post Office and following closure the building has been converted for solely residential use.

63. Portskewett c.1930.
A view from the Crick Road junction looking east into Portskewett village. The complex of farm buildings shown in the centre of the photograph are currently undergoing conversion into residential properties (2007), whilst the church of St Mary the Virgin can be seen on the higher ground amongst the trees to the right side of the scene.

64. Portskewett c.1930.
A view from the churchyard gate looking west. The grass island dividing the roads to Crick and Caldicot has long since gone - a victim of various road widening schemes.

65. Portskewett c.1910.
The *'Portskewett Inn'* with the former village school to the right of the photograph. Concerning the school Kelly's directory of 1901 includes the following details: *'National School (mixed), built in 1876, and enlarged in 1895, to hold 91 children, average attendance, 78. Miss Mary A. Smith, mistress.'* In recent years the school has relocated to purpose built premises at Crick Road and is now called *'Archbishop Rowan Williams Church in Wales Primary School'* and it has replaced both the former Portskewett and Sudbrook schools.

66. Portskewett Church c.1935.
This original postcard was published by Jenkins & Evans of Portskewett Post Office and shows St Mary's church clad in ivy. Today the church has a rather different appearance having been fully renovated in recent years including returning the exterior stonework to its original rendered and lime washed finish, as was the ancient practice in many churches in parts of Wales. The church is mostly Norman with massive walls and a Norman chancel arch. It consists of nave and chancel, a tower at the west end and a large porch on the south side. It is considered to be one of the best examples of early architecture in South Wales. In the north wall are the remains of what is thought to have been a priest's door, and over it is a massive stone with Greek-shaped cross cut into it.

67. Portskewett Station c.1910.
Passengers could catch trains here for Chepstow and Gloucester or Newport, Cardiff and beyond. However much of the activity at the station was centred on commercial traffic at a time when most local traders relied on the railway for both delivery to and from their businesses. Here is a typical scene including the cart and horse of Hobbs & Sons.

68. Portskewett Station c.1920. A goods train at Portskewett station. The original station was located close to the bridge that carries the road to Sudbrook from where a single track line was laid to facilitate the construction of the Severn Tunnel. However, the station was later moved to a site which today is adjacent to Station Road and Hill Barn View.

69. The Walker Memorial Home c.1917.
The Walker Memorial Home (in memory of Thomas Walker chief engineer of the
Severn Tunnel) was located on the very edge of the grounds of Caldicot Castle
opposite the *'Castle Gate'* business centre of today. Dr and Mrs Cropper of Mount
Ballan gave the home (previously used as an orphanage) over to the war office for use
as a military hospital for convalescing troops. Here is a scene from the height of World
War One showing the Red Cross staff and some of the patients.

70. Sudbrook village c.1900.
Sudbrook, although the site of occupation since the Iron Age is best known today as a
Victorian industrial village, created to house the workers involved in the construction
of the Severn Tunnel. People flocked from all parts of Great Britain (and beyond) to
seek work on the project. A community quickly grew up and included such facilities as
a mission hall to hold 250 people together with a day school and a Sunday school. Road
links were improved, encouraging tradesmen from Chepstow and Caldicot to sell
provisions to the new community.

71. Sudbrook village c.1885.
An early street scene at Sudbrook where construction of the first houses had begun in the 1870s with further building taking place throughout the first half of the next decade to house the ever increasing workforce. Several houses were built which also gave additional provision for lodgers, plus houses for the managers and a large house for the foreman of the tunnel, Joseph Talbot.

72. Sudbrook Mission Hall c.1880.
Thomas Walker was a very religious man and one of his first acts at Sudbrook was to erect a mission hall. The mission room that Walker built was designed to hold 250 people but due to the enlarged workforce at Sudbrook, the partitioning walls of the schoolrooms were removed so that the mission room could now hold 400. By the middle of November 1882 however, the number of people regularly attending the room was often 500 and although Walker had planned to enlarge the mission room, its close proximity to the school made this difficult. In addition, the day-school was also crowded, but on the night of the 26th of November, a fire totally destroyed the mission room as well as an American organ and several books. The morning after the fire, Walker sketched the plans for a much larger replacement to be built on part of the three acres of land that he had leased for building houses. Working day and night, often in frosty weather, but with the benefit of electric lamps, the new mission hall was completed on the 16th of December and the first service in the 1,000 seat hall was held the following day.

73. Sudbrook village c.1906.

Disaster struck the Severn Tunnel project on October 16th 1879 when with a mere 500 feet remaining between the meeting of the two shafts, the team excavating in a westerly direction hit the *'Great Spring'* and thousands of gallons of fresh water flooded into the workings. Prior to Thomas Walker's appointment, in order to pump the shafts dry, the Great Western had ordered two massive pumps and together with the existing pumps in the main workings could remove 460,000 gallons per hour. Walker's first task therefore was to build the two engine houses which would serve these two pumps; one house would contain six boilers, the other seven. This work would take about six months to complete without any possibility of work continuing underground until after this time. These two engines were of massive proportions. Built by Harvey & Company of Hayle in Cornwall, the larger of the two engines utilised a steam cylinder of 75 inches in diameter topped by a 30 feet beam weighing 23 tons. Working at eight strokes per minute, this pump alone raised 3,000 gallons every minute.

74. The flooded Severn Tunnel workings c.1883.
In 1883 the Severn flooded and the cuttings for the construction of the Severn Tunnel were flooded. This is the highest flood that has been properly authenticated. The chairman of the Great Western Railway, Sir Daniel Gooch, wrote in his diary: *'So high a tide has not been known for a hundred years.'* The flood was so memorable that it was commemorated by an iron plate affixed to Chepstow Bridge.

75. Severn Tunnel entrance c.1886.
Here pictured shortly before opening, final works are being completed to the cutting at the entrance to the tunnel. On the 1st of September 1886, the tunnel was opened for goods traffic, and was inspected by Colonel Rich, the Government Inspector on the 17th of November with a view to opening for passenger traffic. Nearly fourteen years from the time that the Great Western commenced the works, the Severn Tunnel was opened to passengers on the 1st of December 1886.

76. Sudbrook Brick Works c.1882.
The huge amount of construction materials required for both the tunnel itself and the building of the new village necessitated the need for a local brick works. Here pictured is an 1882 version of a heavy goods vehicle!

77. Holy Trinity Church, Sudbrook c.1910.
Holy Trinity Church (often referred to locally as Sudbrook Chapel) has been a ruin probably since the 18th century when it was abandoned perhaps because the former strategic importance of this site had diminished. In earlier times this had been the location of an Iron Age fort and later a Roman camp - indeed the church is located within the confines of these sites. From here a watchful eye could be kept on the Severn in case of invasion from an enemy sailing upstream.

78. Black Rock c.1883.
Pictured at the Black Rock Hotel are the workers from the Severn Tunnel who no doubt were very thirsty after a hard day's work, quarrying and digging.

79. Sudbrook 1909.
Here pictured is military activity of a more recent kind at Sudbrook Camp (the terraces of houses can be seen in the background). In the years leading up to World War One troops often camped and trained here. Here they are pictured enjoying a tug-of-war.

80. Sudbrook 1920.
The peninsula at Sudbrook gives easy access to the Severn Estuary and photographs of visitors *'taking the sea air'* are common. Here's such an occasion sometime around 1920.

81. Sudbrook c.1930.
And here's another. Fashions have changed somewhat and the style of the ladies' hats indicates that this photograph dates from around 1930. Sadly the names of the group members are unknown. Perhaps local readers can help identify some of them?

82. Sudbrook late 1930s.
And one more! Fashions have changed still further and whilst ladies' skirts have got shorter, a shirt and tie is still the order of the day for gentlemen! The two young ladies pictured here are Olive Arthur and Elsie Fitzgerald.

83. Black Rock c.1879.
A lithograph print of Black Rock viewed from the ferry. At Black Rock there was a large timber pier, which the train ran right out onto, before passengers got off and made their way down the steps onto the ferry boats. A rather frightening arrangement for even the most experienced of travellers! The pier mysteriously caught fire on 22nd May 1881 and was totally destroyed. Some people were quick to blame the Severn Tunnel workers from Sudbrook who at the time were involved in strike action over the length of their shifts, but Thomas Walker the chief engineer defended their innocence. The ferry service ceased with passengers having to use the Beachley to Aust option instead.

84. Sudbrook Football Club. Late 1950s.
Pictured left to right: Back row: Jack Cook, Mr Vickery, Terry Hodges, Tony Stephens, Mr Hughes, Colin Harrison, Arthur Coles. Front row: Malcolm Thomas, Eric Price, Michael Hodges, Ernie Taylor, Les Corfield, Michael Harrison.

85. Sudbrook c.1938.
Pictured here are members of Sudbrook Health and Beauty Club. Sadly no more details have been established.

CHAPTER 3

Roggiett & Llanvihangel

86. Roggiett c.1910.
A general view of the village from the railway sidings. The Roggiett Hotel can be seen in the centre of the view, whilst to the left in the distance is the tower of the parish church. By 1901 Roggiett had expanded hugely, transformed from a sleepy agricultural settlement into a railway village including the building of many new houses for the railway workers, including those at Sea View Terrace pictured here.

87. St Mary's Church, Roggiett c.1900.
Pictured here ivy clad St Mary's Church with Manor Farm in the background. The church is an ancient building presenting several features of interest, consisting of an unusually large chancel, nave, south porch and a western tower with a peculiar octagonal pinnacle at one corner and containing one bell. A considerable portion of the fabric belongs to the decorated period, but there are traces of Early English work. There are remains of the stairs to the ancient rood loft. The registers date from the year 1750. The church is maintained in excellent condition by its loyal members and in recent years the fabric has undergone extensive restoration and repair.

88. Roggiett Methodist Church 1933.
Roggiett Methodist Church pictured here at its opening on 30th June 1933. However the existence of a Wesleyan (later Methodist) mission meeting room is recorded in 1901 when meetings were held every Sunday afternoon. The chapel was (and still is) served from Caldicot.

89. Roggiett Methodist Church 1933.
Another photograph from the opening of Roggiett Methodist Church on 30th June 1933. Pictured left to right are: Mr. Coles, Mrs. Coles, Rev. Law, Teddy Thomas, Bill James, Rev. Hearle and Rev. Waterhouse.

90. Llanvihangel near Roggiett 1908.
The tiny hamlet of Llanvihangel near Roggiett (the population in 1891 was 86) has its own church dedicated to St Michael and All Angels, consisting of chancel, nave, south porch and a lofty embattled western tower containing a pre-Reformation bell. The church formerly had a north aisle, taken down about 1830, when two fine recumbent figures were discovered. These figures now lie within the main body of the church whilst the north aisle was re-instated in 1904 when the church was fully restored under the patronage of Lord Tredegar. The church closed for worship in the early 1970s, but occasional burials still take place in the churchyard.

91. Roggiett c.1935.
Roggiett maypole dancers including Joyce James pictured second from the right. In the background can be seen the houses at Westway and neighbouring streets which at this time had only just been completed.

92. Roggiett 1947.

This photograph is entitled *'November 1947 - Birthday honours for Mrs E.E. Sparks - 50 years in the Labour movement'*. On completion the complex of old age pensioner's bungalows at the junction of Caldicot Road and Station Road were named after Mrs Sparks who had served Roggiett as a parish councillor for many years.

93. Roggiett 1925.

Roggiett School AFC including G.H.Baker, Alf Holloway, Trevor Tapp and Reg Massey.

94. Roggiett c.1938.
The cast of Roggiett and District Operatic Society pictured at the end of their 1938 production.

95. Roggiett School 1936.
Pictured left to right are: Back row: Mrs Powell, Katherine Rakes, ? , Sylvia Lewis, Barbara Sheppard, ? , Barbara Keeble, Barbara Moore, Doreen Lewis, Beryl Williams, Mr Baker (Headmaster). 2nd row: Billy Robbins, ? , ? , Kitty Dodd, Nancy Lane, Ruby Curtis, Jesie Titley, Joyce Bullen, Gwen Williams, Gerald Picton. 3rd row: Jackie Pugh, Ted Willis, Paddy Cornaby, David Powell, ? , Arthur Hawker, Roy Clemo, Pat Daniels, David Hughes. Front row; Vernon Lewis, Eric Facey, Roy Thomas, Henry Olif, Cyril Prior, Ken Hawker, Archie Grainger, ? , Arnold Cheeseman.

96. Roggiett Church School c.1931-32.
Amongst others pictured are Headmaster Mr Baker (left) and Mr Ralph Hodges (right).

97. Roggiett Secondary Modern School 1950s.
Forms 5 and 6 pictured left to right are: Back row: John Squibbs, Michael Jones, Walter Cook, Desmond Powell, Terry Rogers, Ken Jones, Richard Key, Ian Edwards, Brian Abbot. Second row: Mr Eric Blackaby, Primrose Morgan, Joan Morley, Joan Cullimore, Marie Dally, Ruth Owens, Pat Smith, Margaret Crook, Mr Morgan. Seated: Mr Rogers, Maria Godwin, June Phillips, Audrey Baker, Maureen Jones, Marcia Darke, Margaret Watts, Miss Davies.

98. Severn Tunnel Junction 1958.
A train arrives at Severn Tunnel Junction heading for Newport and Cardiff on 21st May 1958.

99. Severn Tunnel Junction 1950s.
Here travelling in the opposite direction is a goods train with the busy marshalling yards of Severn Tunnel Junction just visible in the background.

100. Severn Tunnel Junction 1959.
Pictured here is a 'Castle' class 7010 locomotive towards the end of the steam era.

101. Severn Tunnel Junction c.1920.
The station platforms and buildings viewed from the railway bridge. The condition and appearance of a station was a matter of personal pride to the local station master. It is recorded that Thomas Strange was station master at Severn Tunnel Junction in 1901.

102. Severn Tunnel Junction c. 1920.

A superb photograph showing how in the early days of motoring, cars would be driven onto a specially designed truck, for transportation through the Severn Tunnel to the West Country and Bristol. This avoided the lengthy delays and the often unreliable ferry crossing from Beachley to Aust. This service continued to operate until the opening of the first Severn Road Bridge in 1966. When the service ceased in 1966 the cost of transporting a car through the tunnel was 17 shillings (85 pence) compared to 9/6 (47$\frac{1}{2}$ pence) for a car to cross via the ferry.

103. Severn Tunnel Junction 1909.

Pictured are members of the 1909 Severn Tunnel Junction improvement class. Sadly it has been impossible to trace the names of any of the individuals. How many different sorts of hats can you spot?

104. Severn Tunnel Junction.
An undated photograph believed to be from the 1920s. Here are members of the Severn Tunnel Junction staff looking resplendent in their smart uniform. Amongst them is George Jamer (back row, right).

105. Roggiett 1926.
Railway employees pictured at *'The Retreat'* during the 1926 General Strike. Bill James is pictured in the back row (5th from the right).

106. Severn Tunnel Junction.
Railwaymen pictured at Severn Tunnel Junction possibly during the 1950s. The
occasion is unknown.

107. Severn Tunnel Junction Engine Department staff.
Pictured here sometime during the First World War are the staff of the engine
department. Left to right are: Back row: Archie Harry, Jim Ford, Tom Morgan,
Leonard Jones, Alf Carter, Ernie Woods, Ivor Hawthorn, Jim Chalker, W. Jones. Front
row: Kate Knap, Gladys Warrilow, Frederick Warrilow (Deputy Master), Dorothy
Seadon, Annie Hughes, Edgar Bold.

108. Mr R W George JP.

Mr George was a sometime station master of Severn Tunnel Junction. He is pictured here at his home Prospect House, Chepstow Road, Caldicot.

109. Severn Tunnel Junction.

This undated photograph of Severn Tunnel Junction employees shows (left to right): Inspector Jack Davies, Glyn Taplin, Thomas Seyes, Garfield Arnold, Graham Webb, Viv Smith and William James.

CHAPTER 4

Magor & Undy

110. Undy and Magor c.1920.
A multi-view postcard illustrating various scenes of Magor and Undy including Magor and Undy churches, the Baptist chapel and various scenes from around the villages.

111. Magor Square February 15th 1910.
Magor Square was often the meeting point for the local hounds particularly when they travelled from other areas and arrived by train at Magor Station. Often they were here at the invitation of Lord and Lady Rhondda at nearby Llanwern Park. Pictured here must have been one of the first and only motor cars in Magor and already parking in The Square is becoming a problem!

112. St Mary's Church, Magor c.1922.
Magor church seen from the south-west. This picture clearly shows how the church is located on considerably higher ground than that in the foreground. Indeed part of a rock face can be seen and might be connected with the origin of the place name 'Magor' which derives from an early word for 'wall'. Land disturbance caused by excavations for the construction of the railway line meant that the difference of ground level is now less obvious, but those people who have ever attempted to dig in the churchyard will clearly testify to the large amount of rock that's located just below the surface!

113. View from the tower of St Mary's Church, Magor c.1920.
Other than Magor House and the range of farm buildings (some of which survive at the junction of West End and Redwick Road) this view clearly shows how small Magor was until the housing developments of the late 20th century. Today the fields here are the location of Blenheim Avenue, Queens Gardens and Kensington Park and other streets. In the background the distinctive shape of Wilcrick Hill can be seen. This was the location of an Iron Age hill fort - an excellent defensive location from which to view the surrounding levels and the Severn Estuary.

114. Magor Square c.1900.

The sleepy heart of Magor village pictured here at the dawn of the 20th century. Magor House is pictured on the immediate left, whilst the Baptist Chapel beyond has its pre-1906 restoration appearance. A Baptist Church is recorded in Magor as early as 1812 when members met at the home of Mrs. Mary James and Thomas Evans was named as the minister. However on 22nd May 1817 a petition was made for the building of a Baptist Chapel called Ebenezer, William Jones, Thomas Leonard and Edward Morgan being the petitioners. The request was endorsed on 28th August 1817. An early paraffin street light marks the spot where many years later the distinctive war memorial would be erected.

115. Undy and Magor c.1938.

A general view of Magor and Undy taken from Mill Common. A coach heads out of the village on the former route of the main road which threaded its way through Magor village via The Wheatsheaf Inn. As can be seen agriculture was still an important aspect of local life with farms located at the very heart of the village. Today the land in the foreground is the site of a housing estate also called Mill Common. This postcard was sent to a Mr. Brace who was evidently recovering in The Chepstow and District Hospital. *'Hope this won't make you feel homesick'* ... *'Hope you will soon be back on the farm'* says the writer.

116. Magor c.1905.

A scene outside the Wheatsheaf Inn showing the old chestnut tree (for many years a feature of this road junction) and the former Cross Farm. This road has at different times been described as Undy Road and perhaps more interestingly Mill Pond Road.

117. Magor c.1906.

Magor Post Office has long been a central focus for village life. This 'listed building' still serves as the village Post Office and shop today. Here the proprietor is named on the signage as J. Griffiths. The post box appears to have been located in the lower pane of the left hand window. This postcard was sent from Magor to Miss A. Edmonds, Rose Villa, Redwick.

118. Magor c.1912.

A rare and interesting view of Magor Village centre. Magor House is pictured here on the immediate right and the properties on the immediate left and West End Farm in the background have survived in spite of road widening. However the second building on the left side (and the adjacent store) were demolished in 1964 and today the principal car park for Magor Square occupies the site. This building was the Church House Inn described by the late Fred Hando as '*the county's finest small Tudor house*'. The Tudor stone mullioned windows can be clearly seen in this photograph. The fireplace, stairs and some tiny windows are preserved on the elevation facing the car park. As well as the Church House Inn and also the Golden Lion and The Wheatsheaf of today, Magor originally had a fourth inn - The New Inn - which was located between The Golden Lion and the Baptist Chapel.

119. Magor c.1957.
Pictured here is Magor Baptist Chapel which retained this appearance for the greater part of the 20th century until alterations in the 1990s, although great care was taken to retain the overall character of the building whilst providing a comfortable and up to date worship area inside. Magor has enjoyed a Baptist presence for almost two hundred years.

120. The Mill Pond c.1934.
Today traffic thunders through the foreground on this photograph. The cottage pictured is *'Pond Cottage'* which remains today and is situated on the junction of the main B4245 and Dancing Hill. The possible early location of a mill, where Morgan's Garage stands today, may give some indication as to one of the original reasons for a settlement here and has clearly given rise to the name *'Mill Pond'*. Indeed in more recent times Hunt Brothers & Williams saw mills were located here and the waters of the Mill Pond drove a waterwheel and provided power for the machinery.

121. The Mill Pond c.1922.
A large pond at the centre of the village wasn't just for powering local industry - an afternoon spent punting on the lake was also an option!

122. Magor School 1922.
Magor School celebrates its 150th anniversary of foundation in 2007 and was originally built as a national school and designed by architects Pritchard & Seddon. Here pictured is group II of 1922: Back row: Ralph Norgrove, Trevor Norgrove, Ivor Jones, ? , Bert Waters. Middle row: ? , Millard Bushel, Elsie Edmunds, Ruby Hill, ?, ?, George Williams. Front row: Marjorie Friend, Dora Gunn, Dorothy Cox, Betty Woods, Joyce Woods, Dora Hill. Helper on left: Muriel Gunn Teacher: Miss Aycliff.

123. Magor School 1940.
Pupils of Magor School pictured here in 1940 with the east window of St Mary's Church visible behind them. Evacuees from London and other major cities swelled the numbers at the school hugely. No doubt amongst the pupils pictured here are some of those children.

124. Magor, early 1940.
Here gathered for a group photograph at the rear of the Baptist Chapel are the evacuees from London, brought to the relative quiet and safety of Magor during the Second World War.

125. Magor Station c.1905.
Quite a good number of passengers waiting for the next train to arrive at Magor! The elegant station buildings and lamps are now just a distant memory for a few folk. Frederick Samuel Ruxton was listed as being the stationmaster in Kelly's trade directory of 1901. The station closed to passengers in 1964 and to goods traffic a year later.

126. Undy Halt c.1960.
Undy Halt was located next to the main road, in front of what is now a vets practice. The halt opened in September 1933 and closed in November 1964. Here you can see the road and the houses of Undy on the left side of the photo - the train is travelling towards Magor and Newport. There was formerly a level crossing located here, which joined West End, Undy, with the main road. However, it was the scene of tragedy during WWII when three children, evacuated from London and staying at Arch Farm, Undy, decided to take a 'short cut' one morning on their way to school as they were in danger of being late. Sadly, they failed to check the railway line before crossing and two of the girls were killed by an on-coming train. Their joint grave remained unmarked in Undy churchyard for many years, until 2007, when local feeling led to funds being raised to pay for the cost of a fitting memorial being erected.

127. Undy 1957.

It wasn't until the building of these houses in the 1920s that the separate villages of Magor and Undy were effectively linked together. However, confusion over the exact location of the boundary between the two villages seems to have been as much of a problem years ago as it is today! Here the publisher labels this picture *'Undy Road, Magor'*, instead of *'Magor Road, Undy'*, which would have been rather more correct! This part of Undy and all that area between here and Magor was for a long time known as *'The Mill Common'*. Kelly's Directory of 1901 notes *'There is a Wesleyan chapel at Mill Common'*. However as early as 11th January 1814 it is recorded that a petition for the establishment of a Wesleyan Chapel was received and granted for worship at the home of William Smith (farmer), but its location is given as being at Magor.

76

128. Undy c.1950.
Fields and open spaces were still in existence even in the heart of Undy village pictured here in around 1950. This view looks from The Causeway across to the main Caldicot Road as it leaves the village with the terrace of houses at Laurel Crescent visible in the distance.

129. Undy c.1957.
Today this is the location of a busy road junction where The Causeway meets the main B4245 road. The tin shack fondly known by many as *'The Bon Bon'* is clearly visible on the right of the picture. The green traffic island on the left of the picture was formerly the location of an iron bench given to the village to commemorate one of Queen Victoria's Jubilees, but it appears to have been removed by the time this picture was taken. Might it have been scrapped as part of the war effort to collect such materials?

130. Undy 20th June 1956.
The 9.05am Gloucester to Cardiff Central train pictured between Undy and Magor.

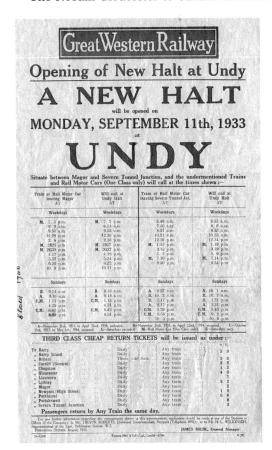

131. Undy 1933.

An advertising poster to announce the opening of Undy Halt on Monday 11th September 1933. Until then villagers had had to walk to Magor station to catch a train. All local destinations are listed along with the fares, but so too are places such as Barry Island and Porthcawl for trips to the seaside which before the railways were only a dream to the majority of ordinary folk.

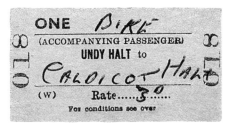

132. Railway ticket 1960.
A railway ticket for a journey between Undy Halt and Caldicot. Notice the price for a bicycle plus an accompanying passenger - Threepence. Note that it's the bicycle that's being charged - the passenger seems just to be an extra!

133. Undy c.1900.
Workmen and two visiting ladies pictured at Undy Quarry. The quarry was located in West End, Undy and the site is still clearly visible today. Quarrying by hand without the aid of explosives or machinery was a hard and dangerous job and although these men could have earned more money by working underground in the coal or slate mines, the working conditions would have been much worse.

134. Outside Undy Church c.1960.
Sadly little detail is known about the reason for this gathering or the names of individuals pictured. Notice the area in the foreground is grassed - today it forms the parking area for the church and the hall, but in former times it was the location of the village pound where stray cattle and other animals were housed awaiting collection by their owners upon payment of a fee.

135./136. Undy 1920s.

Agriculture was the backbone of rural communities in this area and Undy was no exception. Kelly's directory of 1901 states *'The soil is sandy, subsoil, clay, and the chief crops are wheat, barley and hay. The area is 1,763 acres of land and 2,120 of foreshore. The rateable value is £5,398, and the population in 1891 was 393.'* Out of the 23 commercial premises in Undy that Kelly lists, 19 were farms.

137./138. Undy c.1905.

More scenes of farming life in Undy during the early part of the 20th century. The location of these photographs hasn't been confirmed, but it may be The Elms farm which was demolished in the early 1990s to provide the site for homes at St Ann's Crescent and adjacent streets. In 1901 the tenant of The Elms Farm was given as *Hodges - Sarah Ann (Mrs.), farmer.*

CHAPTER 5

On The Levels - Redwick, Goldcliff, Nash, Whitson & Llanwern

139. Redwick church c.1890.
It is possible to see in this view the considerable lean of the church tower towards the east. This is likely to have occurred soon after building was completed in the 13th century and might be attributed to the alluvial nature of the ground in this low-lying area. Even so, masons increased the height of the central tower in the 15th century and it is now a landmark for miles around across the levels. The property whose pine end is seen in the picture was probably ancient, at least in origin, but regretfully was demolished in the late 1940s and much of the rubble was used to provide a base for the newly constructed village hall. Previously the property was a sort of church alms house. The church retains records of income, indicating that it received rent from tenants at the property as late as the 1930s.

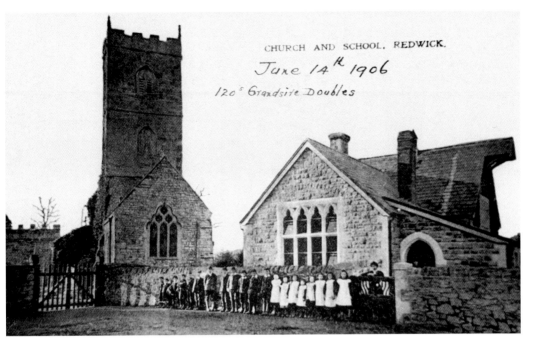

CHURCH AND SCHOOL. REDWICK.

June 14th 1906

120ᶜ Grandsire Doubles

140. Redwick church and school c.1900.

At the heart of this picturesque village, this is a scene that has changed very little during the time since the photograph was taken. Church and school still sit side by side, but the school is now a private dwelling, having closed to pupils in the mid 1950s. The church of St Thomas the Apostle might have at various times had dedications to St Mary the Virgin and before that St Michael and All Angels. However, we can be sure that the church's original dedication was to Thomas - the beautiful silver chalice dating from 1585 bears the name and dedication of the church and confirms the fact for us. This postcard has been written on by a visiting bell-ringer, who records ringing 'Grandsire Doubles' here in 1906.

141. Redwick 1949.

The opening of the new village hall was carried out by Sir William J C Thomas. The chairman of the committee was Mr F Howard James and the secretary was Mr C W Arthur. Mr Hubert Jones commenting in the South Wales Argus said *'I am happy to say that throughout the whole of the works there has never been a dispute. I feel if the country as a whole would pull together as we have in Redwick, we would not be in such a mess!'*

142. Redwick church 1949.
Redwick church was one of the few in this part of Britain to suffer damage as the result enemy action during World War Two. On the night of 5th August 1942 four bombs landed nearby and destroyed a cottage and also damaged the roof and glass of the church. Miraculously although the glass all the other windows was blown out, the east window with its rather good Victorian stained glass survived. After the war, repairs were slow to happen and the church was closed for several years, during which time services were held in the village Baptist chapel, whose members had kindly offered to share their premises. Funding from the war damage commission was eventually forthcoming and after the works were complete the church was re-opened on Thursday 17th March 1949 by Rt Revd Edwin Morris, Lord Bishop of Monmouth.

143. Redwick school pupils 1948/49.
Left to right: Back row: Christine Jones, Clive Millar, Janet Jones, Valerie James, Walter Burroughs, Michael James, Merryl Jones. Front row (seated): Daphne Cowles, Margaret Jones, Len Duffield, Margaret Pask, Kenneth Reece.

144. Redwick village hall 1949.

A grand Redwick tea party in the village hall possibly on the occasion of the opening of the hall. In 1948 Monmouthshire Rural Community Council was allocated funds to build five village halls across the county. Many applications were received, but Redwick was successful and was the fourth hall to open under this scheme. A village hall committee had first been founded as early as 1920 and fundraising began. However, with the onset of the Depression many people left the area to look for work and with the outbreak of World War Two the village abandoned its plans. In 1946 a new group was formed which resulted in the building of the current premises which serves the community to this day.

145. Redwick 1949.
Another photograph from the opening of the village hall. Nearly £1000 was raised by the villagers with another £2000 coming from the Rural Community Council. The contractors were Messrs J Veen & Sons and they were thanked for the personal interest that they had taken in the project.

146. Redwick United Rugby Football Club 1909-1910 season.
This is one of a series of similar photographs of local village teams, taken during the same season. Presumably a travelling photographer was in the area offering special deals to local groups! Pictured (left to right) are: Back row: W Jones, J Cox, J Lewis, R Payne, C P Burris (Hon Secretary). Third row: H Wellington, S Potter, H G Tucker, S Cochrane, W E Baker (President), T L Stead, G H Baker, J Waters, Dr Vaughan, A R Baker. Second row: H Reece, G T Harris, E C Cochrane, J Payne (Vice Captain), J C Reece (Captain), S Reece, T D Pritchard, F Payne, S G Brace. Front row: S Cochrane, H Phillips, A Phillips.

147. Redwick c.1958.
Another Redwick group photo. The occasion is unknown - perhaps readers will help identify some of the faces?

148. Redwick group at Magor Vicarage c.1960.
Until just a few years ago Magor Church fête was an annual August bank holiday event, always held in the extensive grounds of what was then The Vicarage. Each year the Redwick ladies organised a stall and here they are pictured ready and waiting to part the eager crowds from their money!

149. Near Llandevenny c.1947.

We often mistake flooding and changing weather conditions as a curse of the 21st century! Not so - pictured here is a scene near Llandevenny, driving cattle from flooded fields. This area has changed completely with the development of business parks and distribution buildings.

150. Llanwern House c.1910.

Llanwern House formerly located above the village of the same name was built in the late 18th century and over the years was home to several well known local families - the Van's, Salisbury's and later Lord and Lady Rhondda. Like many fine country houses, Llanwern House succumbed to large maintenance and repair bills, crippling taxation between the two world wars and debts arising from death duties. Its end came sometime in the 1950s and now a large set of gates give access to a driveway which leads nowhere.

151. Lady Rhondda of Llanwern

Llanwern House was sometime home to Lord and Lady Rhondda. He was best known as a Minister in the government at the time of the First World War and was responsible for the introduction of food rationing as a policy to assist the war effort. Lady Rhondda was a prominent member of the local Red Cross movement - indeed Llanwern House was requisitioned during World War One as a Red Cross hospital. Lady Rhondda was certainly not a reluctant hostess, rather she actively engaged herself with the running of the hospital and the care of the injured soldiers. Lord and Lady Rhondda are buried only a short distance away in the churchyard of St Mary's church, Llanwern.

152. Llanwern House 1918.
A group picture taken during March 1918 when Llanwern House was being used as a Red Cross Hospital.

153. Llanwern House 1918.
Another group picture this time taken during February 1918. Several soldiers are dressed in their military coats and hats whilst others appear to be wearing a standard outfit for those recovering at the hospital. Notice that several men are clearly standing with the aid of crutches and no doubt many others had more serious injuries which prevented them from leaving their beds.

154. Whitson Court c.1905.
Although a poor quality image, this is an important record of local history. Pictured is Whitson Court, believed by many to have been designed by the famous architect John Nash. For many years the home of the Phillips family whose memorials adorn the walls of Whitson Church, it has since had a variety of unusual uses including a time as a convent. This was during the early 1900s and pictured here are the nuns making hay on the lawns. The building of this house (and also Llanwern House) and the major works to the churches at nearby Nash and Goldcliff point to a period of renewed prosperity for the Caldicot levels during the 18th century.

155. Whitson Court c.1906.
Haymaking behind Whitson Court in 1906. Members of the Waters family are pictured along with hired help. Agriculture was for many centuries the backbone of the local economy of the levels. Mechanisation has hugely reduced the number of local people employed in agriculture today, but even so it remains a major factor in the life of the levels.

156. St Mary Magdalene, Goldcliff. c.1900.
Here's a view of Goldcliff church probably pictured around the year 1900. Few burials have yet to take place. Goldcliff was also the location of a Benedictine priory founded in 1133, from where monks worked the levels, digging the reens and ditches we know today and turning the whole area into extremely productive agricultural land. Goldcliff Priory was dissolved by Henry VIII and has been largely lost to the sea over centuries of coastal erosion. Goldcliff church is thought to have originally been a chapelry of the priory. It was founded in the 13th century and was originally just a single cell building. It was restored in the late 1700s as features in the building indicate, but the tower was a later addition, perhaps being as late as 1800.

157. Whitson to Llanwern Road c.1930.
The huge development of the Llanwern steelworks site meant extinguishing or diverting many ancient roads and tracks across the Caldicot levels. Here pictured is one such route. This is the Whitson to Llanwern road, approaching the level crossing to cross the main railway line from the Whitson side. Adjacent is Monks Ditch this being the original causeway to the sea.

158. New House Farm, Whitson c.1940.

Here's another scene which has been totally transformed by industrial development - that of New House Farm, Whitson, demolished in 1959 by Richard, Thomas & Baldwin, when they built the Llanwern steelworks. The remains of this farm are still visible near Whitson electricity sub-station. Probably originally built around the year 1600, it carried with it the title of the Lordship of the Manor of Whitson.

159. The Great Flood 1607 - A woodcut image.
On 20th January 1606 (or 30th January 1607 in our modern day calendar) a huge flood inundated large parts of South Wales and the West Country. Thousands of people are believed to have died as the waters of the Severn came over the sea wall defences and destroyed homes and drowned people and animals. News soon spread to London and small pamphlets called chap books (the equivalent of newspapers) carried the news and featured illustrations such as this. The 400th anniversary of the *'Great Flood'* was commemorated in 2007 in local villages.

```
                    1606
ON·ĦE·XX·DAY·OF·IANVARY·EVEN·AS·IT·CAME·TO
PAS*IT·PLEASED·GOD·ĦE·FLVD·DID·FLOW·TO·ĦE
EDGE·OF·ĦIS·SAME·BRAS*AND·IN·ĦIS·PARISH
ĦEARE·WAS·LOST·5000·AND·OD·POVNDS·BESIDES
XXII·PEOPLE·WAS·IN·ĦIS·PARRISH·DROVN
*GOLDCLIF { IOHN·WILKINS·OF·PIL·ĦEW·AND
           { WILLIAM·TAP·CHVRCH·WARDENS
                    1609
```

160. The Great Flood 1607 - The Goldcliff Brass.
The Great Flood is commemorated in quite a number of churches on both the Welsh and English sides of the Severn Estuary. At Goldcliff this takes the form of a brass plaque on the north wall of the chancel, inside the church. The plaque, erected by the churchwardens, notes first the financial loss to the parish and secondly the loss of life! In Goldcliff alone twenty-two people lost their lives, representing a huge proportion of a tiny community.

161. Goldcliff United Rugby Football Club 1909-1910 season.
Pictured (left to right): Back row: F E Jones, T A Cox, S G Adams, E Newton, C B James, R J Waters, R G Williams, I T Barrett, J Wright. Second row: E James, E E Waters, S J Roberts (Vice captain), J T Williams (Captain), T P Walters, W Greenhalgh, Lt. Whittaker. Front row: G Whittaker, T H Williams, J B James, C P J Waters.

162. St Mary's Church, Nash. 1897
The large and imposing church of St Mary at Nash has a fascinating and complicated history. Restored to its former glory in 2006, it boasts a wonderful Georgian interior complete with box pews, three decker pulpit, reading desk and gallery. However the church itself is much older, largely dating from the 13th century. Here is a photograph of another phase of restoration work, on this occasion to the tower and spire during 1897, overseen by Messrs Pritchard and Seddon diocesan architects.

June 1906

120's Grandsire Doubles

163. St Mary's Church, Nash c.1905.

This is another view of St Mary's a few short years later. This card was obviously purchased by a bell-ringer who marked it to remind himself that he had rung the bells here in June 1906. The church has a fine ring of eighteenth century bells, five of which were cast by founders Bayley's of Bridgwater, Somerset.

164. Farmfield Farm, Nash c.1935.

A scene depicting a rural idyll, but actually this picture tells the story of the industrial development of the levels. This house probably dated back to around 1700. The Waters family lived here for the last 100 years until the 1950s when it was demolished to make way for the ash ponds, an overflow of ash from newly built Uskmouth Power Station.

CHAPTER 6

Around and About Netherwent - Langstone, Llanmartin, Penhow, Llanvaches, Wentwood, Llanvair Discoed, Caerwent, Crick, St Pierre, Shirenewton, Mathern & Mounton

165. Magor Road, Langstone c.1920.
This rural scene looks out from the rear of The New Inn towards Llanmartin and has changed very little in the intervening years. Ford Farm (pictured centre) is of medieval origin and retains many of its original features. It takes its name from the original ford where the road to Llanmartin crossed a brook which later on its journey towards the Severn becomes Monksditch.

166. St Martin's Church, Llanmartin c.1930.
Originally St Martin's effectively acted as the family church of the Morgan's of Pencoed. Sadly a family chapel attached to the north side of the church became ruinous and was finally demolished in 1858 when the nave, chancel and vestry of the current church were re-built. The west tower - a notable landmark for motorists on the nearby M4 motorway - dates from the 14th century. However, the church contains much of interest for the visitor, in particular the remains of one of the elaborate Morgan family tombs complete with images of a gentleman, his wife, servants and numerous children!

167. Langstone c.1930.

The New Inn at Langstone perhaps just recognisable to some readers, but development of a motel to the rear has altered the building hugely. Notice the early petrol pumps to the left and right of the pub. Obviously this was already a well used route. Today a modern petrol station and shop occupy much of the right section of this view and the road has more than doubled in width!

168. Llanmartin village c.1920.
In this scene, whilst some additional properties have been built, others have been demolished including the former Presbyterian chapel on the immediate right of the picture. All that remains today is the burial ground attached to the former chapel. For many years it was hugely overgrown, but a dedicated team of local volunteers has now cleared it and made access possible again. The road twists and turns in the same way today although it is considerably wider and faster.

169. Llanmartin c.1944.
The Caldicot levels have been a place of military activity over many centuries. Here is a photograph of military activity of another kind - the prisoner of war camp at Llanmartin. Today the Underwood Estate stands on part of the site of the camp, but until only a few years ago the last remnants of storage sheds and outbuildings remained.

170. Pencoed Castle c.1915.
Pencoed Castle might be described as a moated residence rather than a traditional fortress. However it was originally a substantial Norman fortress - the largest between Newport and Chepstow with the exception of Caldicot. The property was re-built in Tudor times into a rather splendid and imposing residence, but later fell into decay. Lord Rhondda began restoring the buildings in 1914, but the task was later abandoned. The castle remains in private ownership. The ruins are clearly visible in this photograph which was taken on the occasion of a visiting hunt group. The hunt were frequent visitors to both here and Llanwern Park arriving in the area by train, alighting at Magor station.

171. Penhow c.1930.
Penhow literally translates as *'the end of the ridge'* an accurate description of the landscape here. The properties to the right of the picture remain largely unaltered although today they are set back from the greatly expanded road which has been re-aligned. However, the shop or petrol station at the end of the row of cottages has long since gone.

172. Penhow c.1930.
A scene from the early days of motoring. For many years this was the principal route from South Wales to the west of England via the ferry crossing at Beachley, Chepstow. The shop on the right of the picture (for many years a Post Office) has now ceased business after some years of 'off and on' trading.

173. Penhow c.1900.
Clearly before mass ownership of the motor car. Evidence of horse drawn transport is confirmed particularly on the road!

174. St Brides School, The Pike, Penhow.
Pictured left to right: Back row: Bob Skinner, John Fletcher, Peter Bennett, George Goulding, Elwyn Harris, Pem Deacon, Ray Edmonds. Third row: Les Viner, K Austin, Owen Stephens, Dennis Humphries, Eric Collingbourne, Len Parkes, Ted Williams, Ken Greening, Bernard Hayes, Raymond Lloyd. Second row: ? , Ted Davies, Eric Beal, Jack Harris, Colin Stead, Gordon Jones, Doug Deacon, Bill Brace, Roy Probert. Front row: Chris Francis, Graham Deacon, Arthur Sainsbury, Dennis Nicholas, Arthur Gibbons, Tom Watts, Doug Humphries, Henry Huckson, Colin Griffiths.

175. Village Farm, Penhow c.1910.
Centrally located within Penhow, Village Farm has 'in outward appearance' at least changed very little over the last one hundred years. Perhaps readers can identify the young lady standing outside the front door?

176. The church of St John the Baptist, Penhow c.1910.
This photograph pre-dates the restoration of the church in 1913 by HJ Griggs of Newport. He re-roofed the church, replaced some of the window tracery and reconstructed the upper section of the tower. The louvred tower openings pictured here are quite different to those of today when a comparison is made. The unusual layout of the church is partly explained by the restricted and steep site. Parts date to the Norman period and others to the 13th century. There is a good selection of 19th and 20th century glass and within the tower are a ring of six bells, the five largest originating from the 18th century Evans family bell foundry in Chepstow.

177. Penhow Castle c.1910.

For many years a tourist attraction and styled as *'Wales' oldest lived in castle'* Penhow Castle is again a private residence (2007). The castle dominates the local landscape standing as it does on a rock premonitory, along with its neighbours the church, the former rectory and a farm. Although of Norman origin, the parts of the castle that remain today date principally from the 13th century. Pictured here is the 17th century extension to the castle a good example of post restoration work retaining period features such as panelled rooms, doorways and fireplaces. This was yet another property that was acquired by Lord Rhondda of Llanwern Park. He bought both Pencoed and Penhow castles in 1914.

178. Llandevaud Country Home for the Blind c.1908.

The Newport and Monmouthshire Blind Aid Society opened a home at Llandevaud in 1902. The Rev James Swinnerton was an influential figure in its founding and was himself incumbent of Llandevaud from 1897. Later workshops offering employment for the blind were also opened. The home was closed about seventeen years later. Swinnerton's interest in the cause of education and employment for the blind may have begun in 1898 when the Rev Thomas Barnard, himself blind, was ordained deacon and appointed curate to James Swinnerton at Llandevaud. He also assisted Swinnerton in his work for the Church Pastoral Aid Society and married his only daughter in 1899.

179. Llandevaud Country Home for the Blind 1909.
Here are pictured the Monmouthshire Blind Workers Association and visitors at Llandevaud Country Home on August 31st 1909.

180. Llanvaches Church c.1900.
Llanvaches is named after St Maches a Celtic maiden who is said to have been extremely beautiful, but was brutally murdered on this spot and this church was founded in her honour. Nowadays dedicated to St Dyfrig, the 14th century church has been restored on several occasions the last being in 1907-08 at the expense of Viscount Tredegar. Extensive repairs have been carried out in recent years to preserve the building for future generations.

181. Tabernacle Chapel c.1900.
Besides the modern A48 stand the early 20th century chapel and hall, the latter dated 1924. They are successors of the first dissenting chapel in Wales, convened in 1639 by William Wroth who had himself resigned as rector of Llanvaches the previous year following a dispute with the established church and the bishop of Llandaff. Wroth was a charismatic minister and enjoyed widespread local support, although he himself had always wished to continue the struggle for reform from within the church and had no wish to be considered a dissenter.

182. Wentwood Reservoir c.1900.
This early photograph of the reservoir is taken from above the Wentwood road and clearly shows the castellated valve tower with its corbelled walkway which dates from the late 19th century. However construction of the reservoir began as early as 1840 and was created to supply water to the rapidly growing town of Newport.

183. Wentwood c.1905.
Little is known about this scene of apparent rural bliss other than it clearly shows The Rose Gardens, Wentwood. Perhaps readers might have more information about the location of this property and know something of its history?

184. St Mary's church, Llanvair Discoed c.1905.
This is one of a series of postcards published by W Lewis of The Post Office, Llanvair Discoed, in about 1909. Here pictured is the parish church of St Mary's from where the village gets its name - Llanvair Discoed translating as *'the church of St Mary below the wood'* the *'wood'* in question obviously being Wentwood. St Mary's church although of ancient foundation, has been rebuilt at least twice - once in 1746 and again in 1882-83, the later rebuilding only retaining the south doorway and the outer jambs of the porch. The church is most attractive and well cared for and contains an 18th century font, some interesting memorials and a good selection of both 19th and 20th century stained glass.

This stone now serves as a stile separating the road from the Churchyard in the village called Llanvair-Discoed, near Caerwent (*Venta Silurum*), Monmouthshire. Originally, as its verse—

Who Ever hear on Sonday
Will Practis Playing At Ball
It May Be before Monday
The Devil Will Have you All,

would imply, it was fixed in the wall of the church—most probably on the north side of the chancel.

Stile at entrance to Churchyard, Llanvair-Discoed, Monmouthshire. Probably originally in the wall on the North side of the Chancel.

185. St Mary's church, Llanvair Discoed c.1920.
Formerly part of the stile into the churchyard this notable stone tablet was later relocated to the interior of the south porch of the church presumably in an attempt to lessen its weathering and decay. The verse is part of a considerable local reaction to James I *'Book of Sports'* which was re-issued by Charles I in 1633. This allowed *'lawful recreation'* on the Sabbath, something local puritans were deeply opposed to. Indeed this was almost certainly the issue which eventually led the rector of the adjacent parish of Llanvaches resigning his living and forming the first dissenting chapel in Wales.

186. Llanvair Discoed c.1909.
Agriculture was literally at the heart of this village, as this picture to the front of Court House clearly shows! Court House dates from 1635 - or at least its front porch does - an inscription in Welsh on the front confirms this.

187. Llanvair Discoed c.1909.
A considerable number of additional properties now line this road as it climbs the hill. Obviously it was still safe to play in the road at this time - it was to be many years before motor cars would be a regular feature of village life.

188. Llanvair Discoed children's group c.1950.
The occasion and exact date are unfortunately unknown, but a sumptuous tea has been prepared! The flag appears to leave no doubt where local allegiance lies! Perhaps it's a St David's Day tea party?

189. Llanvair Discoed Castle c.1909.
Located above the church these ruins are in private ownership. Evidence points towards a small but well defended castle probably dating from the 13th century. Entry is not permitted, but in winter when the vegetation dies back a reasonable view can be obtained from the western boundary of the churchyard.

190. Llanvair Discoed School c.1950.
Once forming a central and important part of village life the school was opened in 1915, but was closed in recent years and was subsequently demolished and houses built on the site. A productive vegetable garden appears to form part of the school grounds.

191. Llanvair Discoed c.1950.
Again the exact date of this photograph hasn't been established, but the occasion is most definitely the Llanvair Discoed village fête. *'Guess the weight of the sheep anybody?'*

192. Caerwent c.1930s.
A scene at the east gate, Caerwent. The property on the right of the photograph was formerly the police house, whilst the cottage on the left was built into the Roman city walls. It clearly looks derelict in this photograph and was demolished sometime later. Located for many years against the side elevation of the police house was an Automobile Association roadside telephone box.

193. Caerwent c.1925.
These stones were discovered at a depth of about three feet and were raised to the surface and reassembled at the present ground level. Today they form the supporting plinth for the War Memorial, a focal point within this historic village. The patch of grass has long since disappeared!

194. Caerwent 1932.

Frank Drower, village baker and postmaster, commissioned this series of postcards to celebrate the construction of his new Post Office, general stores and bakery in 1932. This view - No. 1 of 5 - features Frank Drower himself, with his 12 year old daughter Marjorie. This scene at the heart of the village is little altered today.

195. The church of St Stephen and Tathan, Caerwent c.1910.
The earliest part of the current building is the chancel dating back to the 13th century. Pictured here is the unique lych-gate. It is a substantial construction lavishly carved and dates from 1902-03. It was built in memory of Thomas A Walker of Mount Ballan, chief engineer of the Severn Tunnel and of numerous other major engineering projects, details of which are recorded on a brass plate fixed to the gate.

196. The church of St Stephen and Tathan, Caerwent interior c.1930.
Originally the church was larger with aisles to the chancel and nave, the latter having been re-created in 1910-12 when the original nave arcade was reopened. The church contains notable items of all periods including Roman artifacts and medieval fittings. The sanctuary was refitted in 1965 by George Pace in his highly effective style and in more recent times the chancel has been successfully re-ordered for present day worship.

197. Caerwent Evangelical Baptist Chapel c.1919.
The chapel has changed little in the intervening years although the white rendering has now given way to rather less sympathetic pebble dash. Sadly the ornate and attractive street lamp to the far left of the scene has long since gone.

198. Caerwent Carnival September 1924.
Little more is known about the details of this picture which was published by Silver of Chepstow. The carnival was a popular annual event in village life and was preceded by a carnival procession including a carnival queen, sometimes a carnival king as well and sometimes court ladies too! The quality of the fancy dress outfits make identification of actual people rather difficult!

199. Caerwent School 1937-38.
Pictured left to right are: Back row: Peggy Jones, Margaret Titcombe, Doreen Harris, Gertie Jenkins, Ethel Jones, ? , Nancy Probert, Christobel Munday, Doris Oliver. Third row: Miss Thomas, Florrie Milne, Ivy Hancock, Rosemary Williams, Joan Reece, Mona Creed, Margaret Griffiths, Mary North, Phyllis Counsell, Doreen North, Elsie Stafford, Mr. Vicarage. Second row: Betty Titcombe, Rose Oliver, Jill Adams, Mabel Counsell, Rita Fuller, Edith Francis, Joyce Powell, Gwen Chappel, Sylvia Stafford, Nesta Creed, Miss Pritchard. Front row: Joan Chappel, Betty Chappel, Lillian Griffiths, Doreen Lewis, Shirley Harris, June Reece, Nora Price, Barbara Titcombe, Nancy Counsell, Phylis Jones, Shirley Adams, Margaret Williams, Nancy Francis, Margaret Hicks.

200. Near Caerwent.
The late Bill Marsh in his recollections about life in Llanvair Discoed and the surrounding area gave the following account: *'At harvest time, these chaps followed the threshing machines around from farm to farm. These machines or 'threshing drums' as they were called, were owned by Mr. E. G. Price of Caerwent House, Caerwent. They were pulled around from farm to farm by steam traction engines, which also provided the drums with power by way of a belt drive from the traction engine flywheel.'* The exact location or date of this scene has yet to be established, but it appears to date from around the time of the First World War.

201. Near Crick c.2000.

Although of no great age this photograph offers a unique viewpoint of Crick and the surrounding countryside. Pictured centre is the M48 motorway winding its way towards Newport crossing the flood plains of the Neddern Brook as it does so. In the foreground can be seen Crick and running across the scene and marked by a line of vegetation is the MOD railway which comes up from the main line at Caldicot and enters the former MOD base at Caerwent. Such was the secrecy of the existence of the (then) naval propellant factory that for many years neither it nor the railway link were shown on any maps.

CRICK MANOR HOUSE, NEAR CAERWENT, MONMOUTHSHIRE

SITUATED about four miles from Chepstow on the main road to Newport, and one mile from the village of Caerwent. An Elizabethan mansion which was converted into a farm-building about a century ago. Within the building may still be seen an ancient fire-place, and the dais reaching across one end of the hall. Several windows have been bricked up, presumably to avoid the window tax. At this house King Charles I. was entertained on two occasions during the Civil War by Mr. Moore, who occupied the mansion at that time. On July 22, 1645, the King came to Crick Manor from Raglan Castle in order to meet Prince Rupert who had crossed from Bristol. A council of war was held, and the King decided to proceed to Bristol by the New Passage at Portskewett. That night the King returned to Raglan Castle, and Prince Rupert to Bristol. Two days later the King paid his second visit to Crick Manor, and narrowly escaped falling into the hands of the Parliamentarians, sixty of whom were pursuing him. Arrived at Crick the King was informed that Bridgwater had fallen, and that His Majesty's person was in considerable danger. The King was advised to send some of his suite forward to Bristol, while the others would conduct His Majesty to Newport. This plan succeeded, for the enemy's soldiers were led to cross the Severn, but His Majesty reached Newport in safety that me night. In the group of farm-buildings may be seen small ancient church of S. Neveyn, now used as a barn, urch existed here in 1119 A.D., and divine service was ·ted at this place down to the seventeenth century.

202. Crick c.1920.

Crick Manor forms part of a group of manorial properties besides the A48 road. It dates from the late medieval period and includes a typical medieval great hall as well as retaining many original window and door openings. The legend as retold on this postcard is that King Charles I came here on at least two occasions at the invitation of the owners, the Moore family. It is said he held a council of war here with Prince Rupert, whilst on another occasion he narrowly missed being captured by a group of sixty parliamentarians who were closely pursuing him. Also within the complex is an ancient chapel dedicated to St Nevern which has been defunct from at least the time of the Civil War and which now forms part of a private house.

203. Shirenewton c.1913.
A rural scene at Shirenewton. The defensive nature of the church's central tower speaks of more troubled times and dates to the 13th or 14th centuries.

204. The church of St Thomas a' Becket, Shirenewton c.1905.
Located at the heart of this popular village, the parish church is viewed here from the west side. Today properties occupy the land in the foreground and mature trees obscure this view of the church. In 1852-53 the nave and chancel were re-built and the north aisle added under the supervision of architect John Norton. The south porch of the church is a notable feature unusually retaining its upper room or parvise. The clock and prominent clock faces to the tower were added later, given in 1918 along with a sixth (treble) bell.

205. Shirenewton c.1920.
Shirenewton A.F.C. - 2nd team pictured with their trainer on this real postcard. Regrettably the names of the individuals are unknown and the date of the photograph can only be guessed at, based on the style of the football kits and the design of the postcard.

206. Shirenewton c.1900.
A wedding photograph taken outside a thatched cottage. Older members of the group are dressed in dark clothes, as was the tradition at weddings of that time. Can readers identify any members of the group or perhaps the location?

207. St Peter's Church, St Pierre c.1905.
The message on the reverse of this original postcard says *'Dear Dick, We shall all be washed away if the weather doesn't alter soon, it really is very serious, all night and again all day today it is raining in torrents...'*. Perhaps things haven't actually changed a great deal! The church at St Pierre is of early foundation and contains evidence of Norman work, but much of the present building dates from the 13th century. There are numerous monuments and plaques amongst them those to members of the Lewis family who were owners of the adjacent mansion from c.1500 to the early 20th century.

208. St Pierre c.1902.
Here at St Pierre the hunt is gathering. The girl on the far left of the picture writes on the back of the postcard - *'can you see me? - I'm talking to the gentleman on horseback.'*

209. St Pierre c.1902.
Here's a scene of life on the St Pierre estate, perhaps at the very end of the Lewis family ownership in the early 1900s. In later years the house became the headquarters of the Scouting movement before becoming the hotel it is today.

210. St Andoenus church, Mounton c.1920.
The tiny church at Mounton is squeezed between a brook and a wooded cliff and enjoys a beautiful and peaceful location. The church is medieval in origin, but what the visitor sees today arises out of a reconstruction in 1880 by architect Walter Evill of Chepstow. There is a good selection of 19th and 20th century stained glass. A former Archbishop of Wales described Mounton church as his favourite from amongst all the many churches of the Monmouth Diocese.

211. Linnet Mill, Mounton c.1935.
The small but often fast flowing Mounton Brook was ideal for powering water mills and many examples were built along the length of the brook including Linnet Mill pictured here. This picture shows the mill long after it had ceased to be used, but during their working lives these paper mills are said to have produced amongst the finest paper available and so it was used for the production of Bank of England notes.

212. St Tewdric's church, Mathern c.1906.
Mathern has long been a significant ecclesiastical location, having been founded as the burial spot of the Celtic warrior Tewdric in whose honour the church stands. The church is larger and more elaborate than many of its neighbours due partly to Bishop John Marshall who re-modelled the church during the period 1478-96. The church boasts a sundial on the south face of the tower, whilst inside are two fonts (one 19th century the other much earlier) and in one window a collection of fragments of medieval coloured glass.

213. St Tewdric's church, Mathern c.1905.
The interior of St Tewdric's church, Mathern. The oil lamps have given way to electric replacements, but otherwise this view remains much the same today. The message on the reverse of this postcard indicates that the writer was from Brynmawr and was enjoying a short holiday during August 1907 whilst staying at Vaynor House, Chepstow. *'Having a lovely time... will be back tomorrow by 8pm train - much love, Auntie'.*

214. Mathern Mill c.1905.
Pictured here is Mathern Mill - very much still in existence and now a private house. Although the chimney stack has long since been demolished, when the writer last saw the property a few years ago it retained all its mill workings on three floors and the remains of its water wheel and race. Mathern Mill became a flour mill later in its life and continued as such until the 1940s.

215. Moynes Court, Mathern c.1920.

Moynes Court was built between 1608-1610 by Francis Godwin, Bishop of Llandaff, but occupies the site of a much earlier property. This property would at the time have been called a lodge house; a compact but well appointed occasional residence for privacy and recreation, away from the principal bishop's residence - Mathern Palace, where all civic and ecclesiastical duties would have been undertaken.

216. The Bishop's Palace, Mathern c.1910.

This was one of the three palaces of the Bishops of Llandaff, although it was the only one left habitable after the rebellion of Owain Glydwr in the early 15th century. The Bishops of Llandaff lived here for some three hundred years, but in the early 18th century it fell out of use and became a farm. Later it was sold to H Avray Tipping the garden designer and since 1957 has been used as a guest house by Richard, Thomas & Baldwins Ltd. and their successors British Steel and today Corus.

217. Bishop William Morgan.

One occupant of Mathern Palace (as Bishop of Llandaff) was Bishop William Morgan. He lived here between 1595 and 1601 after which time he translated to become Bishop of St Asaph. Morgan is well known as the translator of the first version of the whole Bible into Welsh. His achievement is now looked on as a major monument in the history of the Welsh language. It meant that Welsh people could read the Bible in their first language at roughly the same time as their English neighbours had the privilege.

218. Bishop Francis Godwin.

Another occupant of Mathern Palace (as Bishop of Llandaff) was Bishop Francis Godwin who succeeded William Morgan as bishop. Godwin was bishop here from 1601 to 1618 when he became Bishop of Hereford. He had previously been sub-dean of Exeter Cathedral and was a son of a Bishop of Bath and Wells. Godwin published many books in his lifetime amongst which was 'The man in the moone' perhaps the first ever science fiction novel to have been written!

Acknowledgements

Very many people have helped in the production of this book, through their willingness to share information, by the provision of old photographs of the area and through identifying faces, places and dates.

On some occasions it is difficult to determine exact 'facts' and any errors that occur within the text must be considered wholly mine and for these I apologise.

My grateful thanks are also due to Mr. Malcolm Thomas and Mr. Gwilym Davies and all the staff of Old Bakehouse Publications, Abertillery, who have been most helpful in the production of this book.

The author would very much welcome the loan of any further photographs etc. from readers who might wish to see them included in a further volume in this series. He may be contacted at the address of the publishers.

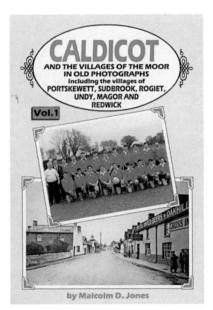

Volume One in this particular series of books was first published in 1995, followed by the first reprint in 2000. Subsequent to this continued popularity, a further reprint is now receiving due consideration.